MW00910619

When Should I Pray?

Little Christian Series

Book 1

Written By: Girmen Rashad

Illustrated By: Mona Mikhail

Copyright © 2007 Elkarez Publishing Company

For permission or ordering information please e-mail requests to **info@elkarezpublishing.com**

I.S.B.N.: 978-1-4276-2821-3

Prepressed & Color Separated by El Karez Graph - Egypt.
E-mail: elkarez@yahoo.com

Printed by St. Mena Monastery Press - Egypt.
E-mail: stminapress@gmail.com

Trust in the Lord with all your heart.

Do not depend on your own understanding.

In all your ways remember Him.

Then He will make your paths smooth and straight.

Proverbs 3 : 5 - 6

When Should I Pray?

Little Christian Series

Book 1

Presented to: _____

By: _____

On: _____

As soon as I wake up in the morning
I should remember to say,

"Dear God, thank you for giving me another chance to show you how much I love you today."

Before I eat my food
I should remember to say,

"Dear God, thank you for sending these blessings my way."

Before I prepare to go to school
I should remember to say,

"Dear God, please help me understand everything I will be taught today."

Before I leave my house
I should remember to say,

"Dear God, please let no harm come my way."

Before I play with my friends
I should remember to say,

"Dear God, please help me win and if don't, that's okay."

Before I go to bed
I should remember to say,

"Dear God, thank you for giving me a special day today."

I should always pray at night...

and during the day.

This is how God will protect me

nd walk with me every step of the way.